THE SCARECROW

by JOYCE and JAMES DUNBAR

A scarecrow stood in a field.
He was lonely.

A robin perched on his sleeve.
'May I build a nest in your hat?' asked the robin.
'Yes,' said the scarecrow, 'but don't peck my head.'

A mouse ran up his jacket.

'May I make a nest in your pocket?' asked the mouse.

'Yes,' said the scarecrow, 'but don't nibble my clothes.'

7

A bee settled on his nose.

'May I make a nest in your boot?' asked the bee.
'Yes,' said the scarecrow, 'but don't sting my foot.'

And a spider moved in without asking.

The scarecrow waited for a while. Then . . .

. . . his hat began to cheep.

His pocket began to squeak.

His boot began to buzz very loudly.

The spiders patched his clothes with cobwebs.

And the scarecrow wasn't lonely anymore.